"Jared Kennedy brings the great Reformer Martin Luther to life—haunted by thunder and lightning, hunted by kings and popes, humbled by our Lord Jesus and his word! But Kennedy does more than retell Luther's full and fascinating story. Like Luther himself, he points readers to Luther's first love: the strong and mighty word of God that does what it says—creating, forgiving, making holy, and giving true life in Jesus Christ. An excellent book for first meeting the boisterous pastor, preacher, and professor of Wittenberg!"
    Todd R. Hains, author, *Martin Luther and the Rule of Faith* and *Who Is Our King?*; editor, FatCat Books

"*The Story of Martin Luther* is a lively tale about a lively man. Jared Kennedy recounts the complexities of Luther's life in a way that is understandable, interesting, and relatable, without oversimplification or condescension. I can think of no better way to introduce children to the Protestant Reformation than by giving them this biography."
    Betsy Childs Howard, Editor, The Gospel Coalition; author, *Arlo and the Great Big Cover-Up*

"Phenomenal. *The Story of Martin Luther* is so much more than a biography. It is perfectly aimed at engaging young readers with exceptional storytelling and compelling narrative, and it is artfully and thoughtfully organized with points of visual interest, compelling illustrations, maps, recap sections, study questions, and a timeline. The young people who engage with this work will not soon forget the rich theology, church history, and maybe even the Latin they're encouraged to scribble in the book itself. But more importantly, they will most certainly be shaped by the beauty and power of the gospel on display and will (Lord willing) begin to see God at work in their own stories as part of their own timeline."
    Abbey Wedgeworth, classical home educator; author, Training Young Hearts series

"Jared Kennedy has crafted a fast-paced, fact-based guide to the life of Martin Luther, suitable for children yet worthwhile for any age. Luther is depicted as a man dependent on divine grace whose life was marked by both faith and failures."
> **Timothy Paul Jones,** C. Edwin Gheens Professor of Christian Family Ministry, The Southern Baptist Theological Seminary

"Jared Kennedy's *The Story of Martin Luther* is perfect for young theologians and will be enjoyed by adults as well. Kennedy writes about Luther in a way that simultaneously informs and inspires readers to treasure Jesus and to have confidence in the word."
> **Jamaal Williams,** Lead Pastor, Sojourn Midtown, Louisville, Kentucky; President, Harbor Network; coauthor, *In Church as It Is in Heaven*

"There are few figures in church history who are more colorful than the Reformer Martin Luther. In this volume, Jared Kennedy does a marvelous job of painting Luther with a glorious palette—showing us his persistent faith, his rigorous theological mind, and his endearing humanness. Kids and adults alike will laugh at Luther's antics and thank God for his courage. The world could use some young Luthers today, and I pray this book will be the instrument God uses to raise up gospel-emboldened boys and girls."
> **Megan Hill,** Managing Editor, The Gospel Coalition; author; pastor's wife; mother of four

"Whenever I see a new children's book by Jared Kennedy, it jumps to the top of my list of books to recommend to parents. This skillful retelling of Martin Luther's life is no exception."
   Robert L. Plummer, Collin and Evelyn Aikman Professor of Biblical Studies, The Southern Baptist Theological Seminary

"This book checks all the boxes: interesting characters, well-told history, and rich theology explained so anyone can understand. Best of all, it makes Jesus and his free grace the hero of the story."
   Jack Klumpenhower, author, *Show Them Jesus*

"As young people mature they need to know the centrality of the gospel and the Bible, both in our theology and our day-to-day lives. This accessible, entertaining, and relatable biography of Martin Luther illustrates the fundamentals of these two precepts extremely well. My children will be reading this book as an essential part of their Christian formation and education."
   Cameron Cole, Founding Chairman, Rooted Ministry; author, *Therefore I Have Hope* and *Heavenward*

The Story of Martin Luther

Lives of Faith and Grace

Edited by Champ Thornton

The Story of Katie Luther: The Nun Who Escaped to True Freedom

The Story of Martin Luther: The Monk Who Changed the World

The Story of Martin Luther

The Monk Who Changed the World

Jared Kennedy

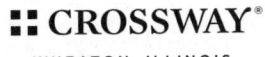

WHEATON, ILLINOIS

The Story of Martin Luther: The Monk Who Changed the World
© 2024 by Jared Kennedy
Illustrations © Crossway
Published by Crossway
    1300 Crescent Street
    Wheaton, Illinois 60187
All rights reserved. No part of this publication may be reproduced, stored in a retrieval system, or transmitted in any form by any means, electronic, mechanical, photocopy, recording, or otherwise, without the prior permission of the publisher, except as provided for by USA copyright law. Crossway® is a registered trademark in the United States of America.

Cover and interior illustrations: T. Lively Fluharty

Cover design: Dan Farrell

First printing 2024

Printed in the United States of America

Scripture quotations are from the ESV® Bible (The Holy Bible, English Standard Version®), © 2001 by Crossway, a publishing ministry of Good News Publishers. Used by permission. All rights reserved. The ESV text may not be quoted in any publication made available to the public by a Creative Commons license. The ESV may not be translated in whole or in part into any other language.

All emphases in Scripture quotations have been added by the author.

Trade paperback ISBN: 978-1-4335-9268-3

ePub ISBN: 978-1-4335-9270-6

PDF ISBN: 978-1-4335-9269-0

Library of Congress Cataloging-in-Publication Data

Names: Kennedy, Jared, 1978- author.
Title: The story of Martin Luther : the monk who changed the world / Jared Kennedy.
Description: Wheaton, Illinois : Crossway, [2024] | Series: Lives of faith and grace series | Includes bibliographical references. | Audience: Ages 8-13
Identifiers: LCCN 2023039221 (print) | LCCN 2023039222 (ebook) | ISBN 9781433592683 (trade paperback) | ISBN 9781433592690 (pdf) | ISBN 9781433592706 (epub)
Subjects: LCSH: Luther, Martin, 1483-1546--Juvenile literature. | Reformation--Biography--Juvenile literature.
Classification: LCC BR325 .K44 2024 (print) | LCC BR325 (ebook) | DDC 284.1092 [B]--dc23/eng/20240401
LC record available at https://lccn.loc.gov/2023039221
LC ebook record available at https://lccn.loc.gov/2023039222

Crossway is a publishing ministry of Good News Publishers.

VP		33	32	31	30	29	28	27	26	25	24
15	14	13	12	11	10	9	8	7	6	5	4	3	2	1

For

Friedrich, Mary Ellen, Fritz, Olivia, and Felix Honay,

and all the families of Leipzig Projekt.

Christ will build his church, and the gates

of hell cannot stand against it.

> "*I simply taught, preached, and wrote God's word. . . . I did nothing. The word did everything.*"
> — MARTIN LUTHER

Contents

1 Thunder and a Vow (July 1505)   *1*
2 Trembling before the Father (1505–1506)   *7*
3 He Went for the Saints (1510–1511)   *17*
4 Coin in the Coffer (1517)   *25*
5 Theologian of the Cross (1517–1518)   *35*
6 I Cannot Recant (1520–1521)   *45*
7 A Bible for the People (1521–1522)   *53*
8 Years of Trouble (1522–1524)   *63*
9 The Estate of Marriage (1523–1534)   *77*
10 Hymns and Catechism (1527–1535)   *89*
11 Chalk on the Table (1529)   *101*
12 Final Words (1530–1546)   *111*
   Conclusion: Lessons from a Life   *121*

   Study Questions   *125*
   Timeline   *133*
   More to Explore   *137*

1

Thunder and a Vow

July 1505

CRACK! A BOLT OF LIGHTNING strikes the earth. Its flash knocks Martin Luther on his back. His bag and belongings fly across the rain-soaked road. *Boom!* Thunder crashes again.

This will be my death, Martin thought.

It was Sunday, July 2, 1505. A day that would

— **GERMAN CITY PRONUNCIATION** —

Augsburg: OWGZ-boork
Eisleben: EYES-leh-ben
Erfurt: AIR-foort
Heidelberg: HIGH-dell-berg
Leipzig: LY-ptsyk

Magdeburg: MAHK-duh-boork
Mansfeld: MAHNS-felt
Marburg: MAHR-boork
Orlamünde: OR-lah-moon-duh
Stotternheim: SHTOT-ern-hyme

Wartburg: VART-boorg
Wittenberg: VIT-ten-berg
Worms: VORMS
Zwickau: TSVIK-ow

Germany's borders have changed since Martin's day. This map shows Germany's present-day borders.

change his life. The week before, the twenty-one-year-old law student had been visiting his parents in Mansfeld, Germany. But as Martin traveled back to the university, he was caught in a deadly storm. The University of Erfurt was only six miles ahead, but Martin wasn't thinking about school.

If Martin had graduated, he'd have been an amazing lawyer. He was smart and good with words, but he wasn't thinking about the money he'd make in a successful law career. He couldn't argue his way out of the storm. There was only one way out. Martin knew his parents wouldn't like it, but in his panic, he bargained with God. *What if I pledge my whole life to serve the church? Will you spare my life if I become a monk?*

Martin knew what becoming a monk would mean. Years before, while at boarding school in Magdeburg, he'd watched what happened when Prince William of Anhalt decided to become a monk. The prince had left his palace, entered the monastery, and taken a vow of poverty. He had been reduced to begging on the streets. "With my own eyes I saw him," Martin later wrote. "I saw him carrying the sack like a donkey. He had so worn himself down by fasting . . . that he looked like death, mere bone and skin."

Why would Martin want to live such a hard life? What could tempt the young man to defy his parents, give away the expensive legal textbook his father had bought him, and forsake a promising career as a lawyer to become a beggar? It wasn't just his fear of lightning and thunder. Other fears raged in Martin Luther's soul.

Martin's father, Hans, was a miner and demanded much of his son. His mother, Margarethe, terrified Martin with the fear of God. She had told him about devils that gather in the dark forest at night. She had warned him about witches that cast spells on cows to dry up their milk. On top of the fears Martin had learned in his family, everyone around Martin thought about death and God's coming judgment all the time. In the 1300s, Europe had faced a massive outbreak of the bubonic plague, the "black death." Nearly a third of the continent's population died.

— Artistic Judgment —

Two woodcut prints, popular at Martin's time, give us a window into the people's fears. One, called the *Dance of Death*, features skeletons summoning people from all walks of life (pope, emperor, prince, child, and laborer) to the grave. Another portrays Christ the Judge sitting on his throne above a rainbow. Lilies extend from his head to the faithful on his right, and a sword extends to the wicked at his left. The message of these images is clear: *Be prepared. Death and judgment can come at any moment.*

Without modern medical advances, people didn't count on living long.

All alone on the road, the warning flashed in Martin's heart like the lightning around him. Psalm 29 says, "The God of glory thunders, . . . The voice of the Lord flashes forth flames of fire" (29:3, 7). Afraid that God the Judge had come for him in the storm, Martin called to the patron saint of faithful miners like his father. Fearing devils might spring from the wood and drag him to hell by his curly hair, Martin cried out, "Saint Anne, help me! I will become a monk."

With those words, Martin committed himself to the only life he believed would guarantee him peace and assurance of final salvation. But what if it didn't? What if becoming a monk couldn't calm the storm in Martin's soul?

2

Trembling before the Father
1505–1506

ONE MONTH LATER, Martin Luther knelt before the altar in the monastery chapel. This was the official ceremony where Martin became a monk. "What do you seek here?" asked the priest leading the service.

"God's grace and your mercy," answered Martin.

The priest next asked, "Are you married?" Martin

had been born twenty-one years before in Eisleben, Germany, on November 10, 1483. He was christened at Saints Peter and Paul Church the next day. Martin was raised as a faithful Roman Catholic. That was the only Christian church that was present in western Europe at the time. Soon after Martin's birth, the family moved to Mansfeld where, at age seven, Martin entered the Mansfeld Latin School. Martin learned Latin grammar and prayers, and he memorized *Aesop's Fables.* Since those early years, Martin had been a diligent student—first in Mansfeld and most recently at the University of Erfurt. While it wasn't uncommon in his day to have a wife by twenty-one, he'd had little time for anything but studying. No, Martin had never been married.

"Do you owe money?" In Mansfeld, Martin's father worked in the copper mines as a smelter (the person who melts down ore to separate the metal from the rock). Martin's dad worked hard, sacrificing to pay for his children's educations. No, Martin didn't owe money.

"Are you hiding a secret sickness?" Martin's entire reason for coming to the monastery was to please God and find grace through his good works. Since his bargain in the storm, he'd been willing to do anything for God's favor. Martin still felt guilt and fear over his sin-sick soul, but he wasn't hiding any physical sickness.

Martin answered no to each question. Then, the priest explained what life as a monk would involve. Martin could never get married, and he would be poor. He'd wear rough clothing, eat simple meals, and fast (that is, go without food) regularly. Martin would have to wake up in the middle of the night for prayer, and he'd work hard at chores throughout the day.

"Are you ready to take up these burdens?"

"Yes, with God's help," Martin declared.

Next, as an act of humility, the crown of Martin's head was shaved, leaving a bald spot called a *tonsure* and a circular patch of hair around the sides.

Last, the monks at the ceremony sang a hymn, and Martin lay down on the floor with his arms stretched out wide in the shape of a cross. From that point forward, Martin committed to a life characterized by self-sacrifice. In all things, he was to think only of God and others, never about his own needs.

Despite this difficult life in the monastery, Martin thrived. He'd been a great law student. Now, he was a diligent monk. He was in a different place, but he was still the same Martin. He excelled at his studies. He diligently kept the routine of the seven daily prayer vigils, and he fasted, sometimes

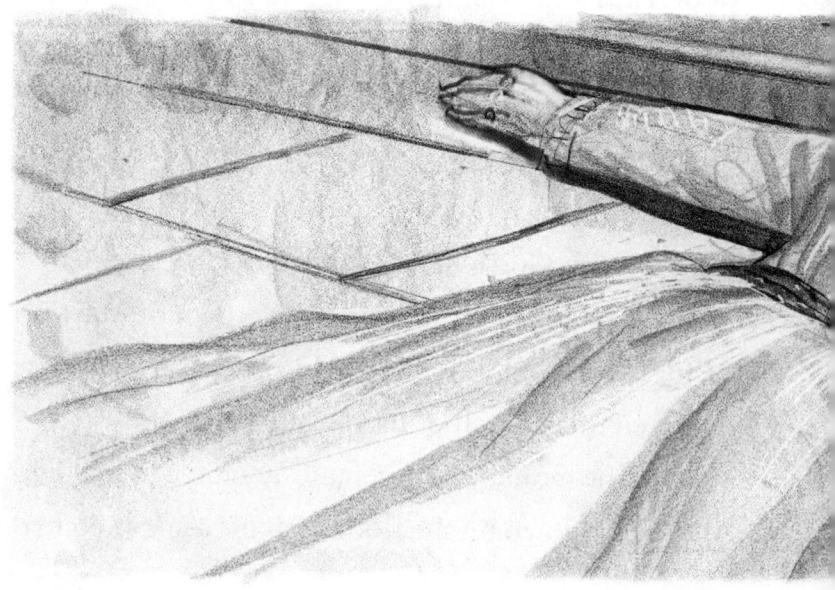

for three days in a row without touching a crumb. "I was a good monk," Martin later wrote, "and I kept the rule of my order so strictly that I might say that if ever a monk got to heaven by his monkery it was I."

That was Martin's goal. He knew that the Catholic Church saw faith and work as the surest path to salvation, and he was confident in this teaching. Confident, that is, until the day he became not only a monk but a priest too.

That was a big day. Martin's father, Hans, came to the service to see his son. He'd been hurt by Martin's decision to enter the monastery, and now that Martin was entering the priesthood, he wanted to put the bad feelings behind them. Hans arrived with a company of twenty horsemen, and he gave the monastery a generous gift of twenty golden gulden, an amount worth three weeks' pay. Hans wanted to make the service into a party for his son.

Martin saw the day differently. The Catholic Church teaches that when a priest serves the Lord's Supper—what they call the "sacrifice of the mass"—the bread and wine transform into Jesus's body and blood. Martin believed that when he held the bread and wine above his head before the congregation, he would be lifting Jesus's actual body.

This scared him. Before the service, Martin prepared by confessing every sin he could remember to another priest. Then, as the service began, Martin took his place at the front of the chapel, and he began to recite the Latin prayers. Martin thought about the theology he'd been studying—*iustitia Dei*, "the righteousness of God" (Rom. 1:17).

God is above all in power and perfection. He's perfect in judgement and completely without sin. As Martin thought about God's righteousness, he recited the service prayer.

"We offer unto you, living, true, and eternal God..."

With those words, terror struck him. *With what tongue will I address such majesty? All people ought to tremble in the presence of even an earthly prince. Who am I that I should raise my hands to God? The angels surround him. At his nod the earth trembles... but I am dust and ashes and full of sin.*

Martin wanted to run away. When he held up the bread and wine, he shook so badly that he almost dropped the cup. Martin leaned over and quietly told the priest assisting him that he wanted to stop.

"No," whispered his friend angrily. "You will continue and quickly."

Though the service was a disaster, afterward there was still a banquet. Martin was still nervous, but he found his dad. He hoped that his father would give him a word of assurance.

Martin asked, "Dear father, why were you so contrary to my becoming a monk?"

A pained look came over Hans's face. He loved his son. The extravagant gifts he'd brought to the service made that clear, but Martin's performance at the mass was a failure. He had nearly spilled the blood of Christ! Hans couldn't understand why his son would become a monk. He'd sacrificed so much so Martin could be a lawyer, but it was all undone by that thunderstorm. Angry and embarrassed, he answered Martin sharply, "You learned scholar, have you never read in the Bible that you should honor your father and mother?"

Martin Luther had botched his first mass. He couldn't please his demanding dad. How could he possibly please God? Perhaps if Martin couldn't, others could do so for him.

— Reading Luther's Latin —

During his school days, Martin learned to read and pray in Latin. Several important Latin phrases appear throughout his writings. After you read about each phrase in the coming chapters, write its English translation below.

iustitia Dei (in chapter 2)	righteousness of God
Crux sola est nostra theologia (in chapter 5)	
revoco (in chapter 5)	
oratio, meditatio, tentatio (in chapter 7)	
Hoc est corpus meum (in chapter 11)	
simul iustus et peccator (in chapter 12)	
extra nos (in the conclusion)	

3

He Went for the Saints
1510–1511

"WHAT DO YOU WANT TO SEE when we get to the Eternal City?" asked Martin's friend. "Do you want to visit the Colosseum? It's massive!"

Martin looked sideways at his friend, then kept trudging through the Alpine snow. Martin hoped his visit to Rome would relieve his spiritual fears, but his friend just wanted to see the ancient city's wonders.

"I hear the artwork hanging in the pope's residence shows beautiful scenes from the Greek and Egyptian myths. Maybe we'll see them when we deliver our report."

Martin's cloister (the monastery house where the monks lived) belonged to a group of monasteries called the Augustinian order. Soon after Martin became a priest, these monasteries were given new leadership. The new priests in charge wanted to make the monks' daily responsibilities less demanding. *Less strict?* Martin must have thought. *If anything, a righteous life requires we do more not less.* To settle the debate, the cloister had sent Martin and his friend to Rome to appeal to the pope. That's what started the two friends on their journey, but Martin had bigger plans for this pilgrimage. Was he walking 700 miles across the Alps, from Erfurt, Germany, to Rome, Italy, to see buildings, monuments, and art?

No, he went to Rome for the saints.

HE WENT FOR THE SAINTS

Why the saints? The Catholic Church taught that when godly saints behave better than they need to, they're able to store up a surplus of goodness in the church's heavenly bank account. To receive a portion of these "heavenly merits" and reduce the consequences due for sin, Christians were told they could earn, or purchase, an *indulgence*. An indulgence was a written certificate used like a coupon for the saints' heavenly merits. Christians could buy these coupons by giving money to the church, or by praying and taking Communion at a sacred shrine dedicated to a saint.

When Martin Luther arrived in Rome, he spent any extra time he had visiting these sacred shrines. He stopped at ones that supposedly displayed the apostle Peter's skull, the finger of doubting Thomas, and the chains that bound Paul while he was in prison. Martin even saw a piece of wood said to be from Christ's cross. Rome had more indulgence shops and shrines to sacred objects (known as *relics*) than anywhere else in the world. During his stay, Martin visited more than he could count.

MARTIN LUTHER

Martin thought going to shrines and buying indulgences would make him more confident and capable of fulfilling God's righteous demands. But the more

> ## — What Is Purgatory? —
>
> Christians during Martin's time believed they could find salvation only if they did more good than bad. Most were able to see the sin in their lives. They knew that when they died, God would need to clean them up (or purge them) before they could enter heaven. The Catholic Church called the purging place *purgatory*, and most people thought they would spend years doing miserable work there until they were holy enough to enter heaven. During Martin Luther's lifetime, the pope said indulgences could be used as coupons for less time in purgatory. These indulgences could be purchased for yourself or for your loved ones. People were thrilled about making their time in purgatory shorter. As a result, the Catholic Church made a lot of money selling indulgences.

Martin saw of Rome, the weaker his faith became. Rome was filled with dirt, crime, and danger. Women couldn't walk through the streets safely. And Martin discovered that most monks and priests in Rome cared more about making money from indulgences than they did about the salvation offered through them.

Visiting priests could lead a mass at one of the sacred chapels in Rome. Martin wanted his service to be meaningful, so to prepare for his chance, he fasted the day before. But when Martin got to the chapel, the front of the church was so jam-packed with young priests waiting in line to say mass and earn heavenly merits that it was hard for him to squeeze himself in. When it was finally Martin's turn, an Italian priest behind him kept whispering for Martin to hurry up and let others have a chance. "*Passa! Passa!*" he urged. "Let's go. Move along!"

Before Martin left Rome, he visited one of the city's most holy places: the *Scala Sancta*. This "holy stairway" is said to be the steps Jesus climbed on his way to stand trial before Pontius Pilate. Wanting to set his grandpa free from purgatory, Martin crawled up the stairs on his knees and repeated the Lord's Prayer on each step. When he reached the top, he felt no comfort. The storm of doubt still swirled within him. He stood up and said, "Who knows whether this works?"

Martin returned to Erfurt sad and despairing. To add to his misery, he was soon transferred away from his friends in the bustling city of Erfurt to the backwater village of Wittenberg. There Martin got to know Johann von Staupitz, the leader of the Augustinian order. Dr. Staupitz was a wise and gentle man, and he wanted to help Martin. Staupitz was convinced that curing Martin of his depression would mean taking the young monk's focus off himself and sending him out to serve others. Years later, Martin would write, "If it had not been for Dr. Staupitz, I should have sunk in hell." But Martin's gratitude for his mentor didn't come right away.

In the fall of 1511, the two men sat under a pear tree in front of the Black Cloister monastery, Martin's new home in Wittenberg. There Staupitz gave Martin

HE WENT FOR THE SAINTS

some unwelcome news. Martin had a new assignment: "You will be a preacher and a teacher of the Bible."

Martin panicked. "I'm not qualified," he said. Then, he rattled off a list of reasons he couldn't do it. Staupitz wouldn't change his mind, so Martin muttered, "Dr. Staupitz, you're going to kill me! I won't survive three months."

The wise mentor wasn't worried. "Well now, in God's name," laughed Staupitz. "If you don't make it, I'm sure our Lord is busy enough that he could use some educated people in heaven too."

From that day on, Martin Luther had a job to do. He would be responsible to teach and care for others. Martin finished his studies, and he joined the theological faculty at the University of Wittenberg and began preaching at the local church the following year. Teaching God's word was Martin's new job, a role that would change both him and the world.

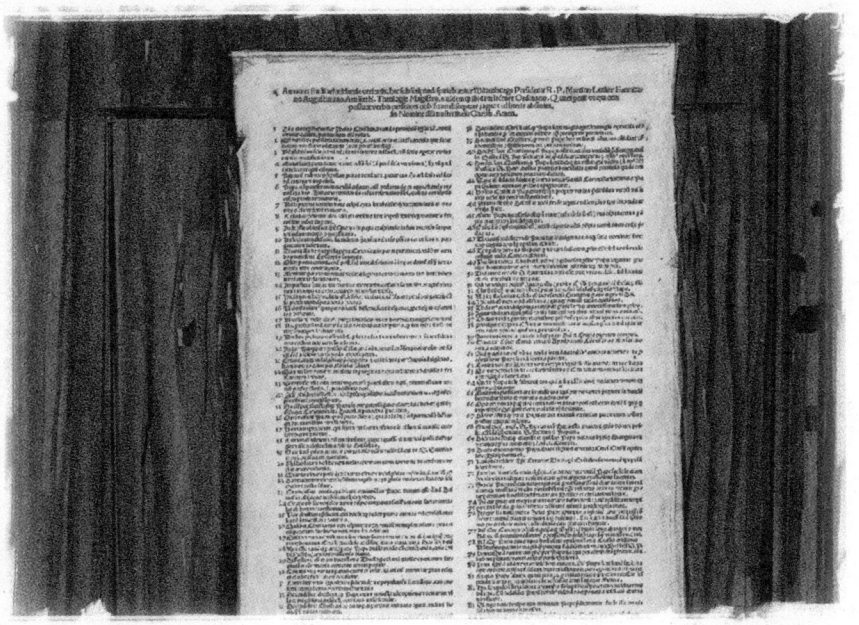

4

Coin in the Coffer

1517

GIOVANNI DI LORENZO DE' MEDICI was the second son of a famous ruler of Florence, Italy. He had grown up in one of Europe's wealthiest and most powerful families. The Medicis ran a bank that loaned money to the kings of England and France and even to the pope. Though Giovanni began serving the church at age seven, it's not surprising—given his family's wealth—that he also enjoyed a lavish lifestyle. Giovanni loved carnivals, art, and feasting, and he continued to love all the comforts money could buy even after he was elected to be the pope.

In that time, kings, queens, and popes often took new names when they received their title and throne. So when Giovanni became pope, he changed his name to Leo X (the Tenth). Though Leo's name changed, his spending habits did not. Pope Leo wasted the church's money on gambling and fancy hunting parties. He loved hunting wild boar so much that he'd wear his long black hunting boots even when he dressed up in his papal robes. (*Papal* comes from the word "papa," meaning father, where we also get the word "pope.") Leo's rich lifestyle and loose spending was a problem for the Catholic Church. The church wanted to spend the money he wasted on more important matters—like building cathedrals.

The church's work wasn't cheap. The man who served as pope before Leo had hired the famous painter Michelangelo to paint the Sistine Chapel ceiling. That pope had also begun construction on a new grand cathedral for Vatican City: St. Peter's

Basilica. It was Leo's job to finish the work, to put the tallest dome in the world on top of the church where Peter was buried. Where would Leo find the money?

The solution was in Germany. Prince Albert of Brandenburg loved power as much as Pope Leo loved riches. Albert was willing to pay for power too. His ambition was to be the highest-ranking church leader, the archbishop, over all Germany. But Albert had a problem. He was too young to hold that position. Albert was smart, though. He knew Leo needed money, so he wrote to ask the pope to bend the rules and let him *pay* for the right to become archbishop.

Leo agreed. So Albert took out a loan of ten thousand gold ducats, a hefty sum even a rich prince couldn't pay back right away. Albert gave that money to the Catholic Church. But Leo wanted more, so he used the shrewd banking skills he'd learned from his Medici forefathers to get it. Leo gave Albert a way both to pay back his loan and to raise more money for the church. He let Albert sell special indulgences throughout his German territories. Whenever someone spent a coin to rescue a soul from purgatory, half would help Albert pay off his debt and half would help Leo build St. Peter's. The more indulgences were sold in Germany, the more both Leo and Albert got what they wanted.

While Pope Leo and Prince Albert schemed for money and power, the anxious monk Martin Luther began his job as a Bible teacher in Wittenberg. Early in his new career, he taught a class on the Psalms. Psalm 22:1 says, "My God, my God, why have you forsaken me? Why are you so far from saving me, from the words of my groaning?" Jesus quoted those words when he died on the cross, but Martin struggled to understand why Christ would say something like that.

Martin knew why he himself felt anguish; he had always felt his guilt before God the perfect judge. When he conducted his first mass, he stood shaking in fear. When he visited Rome, his doubts overwhelmed him. Of course, he felt anguish.

But why did Jesus Christ speak these words? Christ isn't guilty or impure. Christ has no sinful doubts. Why did he feel anguish? The only answer could be that "the Lord has laid on him the iniquity of us all" (Isa. 53:6). What a new vision of Christ this was to Martin! Jesus is still the Judge. He must judge sin as light drives out darkness, but even as he judges, Christ suffers with sinners and gives them his mercy.

The light of God's love had started to shine into Martin Luther's darkness. As he studied and taught the Bible, Martin also began to see what God's word teaches about how sin and guilt are forgiven. Forgiveness can't be earned by entering a monastery. Salvation won't be found by spending hours confessing sins to a priest, by adoring relics, or by making journeys to Rome. Unlike Pope Leo and Prince Albert, Martin began to see that God's grace can never be purchased with money or power.

In 1517, Albert and Leo's money-making plan kicked into action. Prince Albert sent a preacher,

Johann Tetzel, to travel around the German countryside. More than a preacher, Tetzel was an indulgence salesman. He set up preaching stations from town to town, and he used guilt and wild promises to lure people into purchasing indulgences. "Why do you hesitate?" Tetzel cried out:

> Do you have no fear about your sins? Priest, nobleman, wife, and merchant, young and old, are you ashamed to spend a coin on an indulgence but not ashamed to visit a tavern or go to a dance? Your whole life hangs by a thread! Put a coin in the coffer [money chest] and have all your sins forgiven. Don't you hear your dead parents' voices from purgatory wailing, "Have mercy!" When a coin in the coffer rings, a soul from purgatory springs.

When Martin Luther heard about Tetzel's preaching, he was troubled. He saw that Prince Albert was taking advantage of peoples' fears to steal their money and gain power for himself. Martin had to respond. On October 31, 1517, he prepared a document, his *Ninety-Five Theses*. It was a list of ninety-five short statements about repentance, forgiveness, and indulgences. Here is a sample of what Martin wrote:

> 27. They preach only false doctrines who say that as soon as the money clinks into the money chest, the soul flies out of purgatory.
>
> 28. It is certain that when money clinks in the money chest, greed and lust for power can be increased.
>
> 37. Any true Christian, whether living or dead, participates in all the blessings of Christ and the church. God gives this to Christians, even without indulgence letters.

Martin posted these lines on Wittenberg's Castle Church door where all his students would see them. His goal was to get his students thinking and talking about indulgences. He had no idea just how far that conversation would spread.

— Nailed It? —

When people think of Martin Luther, they often think of a defiant monk, enraged by the sale of indulgences. Artists have drawn Martin walking confidently with his hammer in hand to the door of Castle Church where he nailed up his theses in defiant protest of the pope. That's what we envision, but at least part of this picture is a myth.

In Martin's day, nails were very expensive. Before factories, they were made one at a time by a blacksmith. So when professors wanted to post important announcements for their students, they usually pasted them on a door with glue. The first illustrated image we have of Martin with a hammer is from 1697—almost two hundred years after the *Ninety-Five Theses* was written. Why is that the image that's survived? Probably because imagining the Reformer marching through town with a glue pot just isn't as exciting and inspiring.

* To learn more, see Forrest Strickland, "Nailed It? The Truth about Martin Luther, the Ninety-Five Theses, and the Castle Church Door," The Gospel Coalition, October 31, 2022, www.thegospelcoalition.org.

5

Theologian of the Cross
1517–1518

MARTIN LUTHER WAS BOLD. He was only a priest in an Augustinian monastery, a college professor in a tiny town, and a preacher in the local church. But when he posted his *Ninety-Five Theses*, Martin also sent a copy to Prince Albert of Brandenburg, the same prince who had made the deal with Pope Leo to sell indulgences in Germany. The note said, "If you will look over what I've written, you will see how wrong your indulgence doctrine is."

Prince Albert was furious. In anger, he immediately forwarded Martin's letter to the pope. When Pope Leo read Martin's theses, he also acted right away. But Leo didn't think Martin was a threat. He saw Martin as a lowly backwoods priest with no influence. So Leo simply instructed the leaders of the Augustinian monastery to tell the young monk to change his ways. Leo thought this would settle the matter.

He was wrong. Martin's students in Wittenberg had handed copies of his *Ninety-Five Theses* to a printer, and when the paper was published, people across Germany had begun to gather in their homes to read it out loud with their families. They liked the spunky monk from Wittenberg. To protect the weak and poor, he'd spoken up against a prince and the pope.

A few months later in April 1518, Martin wrote another paper, and he prepared to talk about it at the Augustinian order's spring meeting in Heidelberg,

Germany. Martin walked to the meeting in fear, expecting the leaders there to sternly rebuke him, just like the pope had asked. But to Martin's surprise, the priests at the meeting loved his new document. Martin even made new friends at the meeting, and they gave him a ride home. "I went on foot," Martin reported when he arrived back to Wittenberg, "but I came home in a wagon."

What was Martin teaching that got his new friends so excited? In this second paper, his *Heidelberg Disputation*, Martin described two types of theologians. (By "theologian," Martin didn't just mean people who work as Bible teachers for their jobs. He knew every Christian is a theologian because all Christians study about God.) In his document, Martin contrasted two types of people—the "theologian of glory" and the "theologian of the cross." These two types of people have two very different ways of thinking about God.

Theologians of glory think people are capable and smart enough to know God through human reason.

These people say we just need a little help—a little boost from God's grace through the sacrifice of the mass—to live a good and righteous life. They also say we can know who God's righteous people are because we see God reward them with power, success, and wealth. (Sounds pretty glorious, right?)

— Luther and the Printing Press —

Johannes Gutenberg invented the moveable-type printing press around 1440. One hundred years later, Martin Luther made book publishing a force to be reckoned with. In 1500, German presses were only printing about forty German books per year. After all, only 3 to 4 percent of the German population could read. Everything began to change when Martin came on the scene.

Martin's rejection of indulgence sales and the pope's authority was a sensation. In his writings, Martin said the common people could form their own opin-

THEOLOGIAN OF THE CROSS

Though Martin didn't use Prince Albert and Pope Leo's names, it's clear he was talking about their greedy doctrine of indulgences when he described the theologian of glory.

Martin's "theologian of the cross" was different. This person knows that the truth can't always be

> ions about the issues being debated if they'd just read the arguments for themselves. That's what people began to do. Families gathered around books and pamphlets and sounded out the words, eager to discover what Martin Luther and his opponents would write next. In 1523, printers published 498 German titles. Martin wrote 180 of the books.
>
> It was like what happened with the smart phone more recently. The printing press was a new technology, and when Martin's books were printed, he became as famous as social media influencers are today. As a result, the way people thought and communicated completely changed.

judged by outward appearances. It's not always people who appear good, beautiful, and powerful by worldly standards who truly know God. (After all, Jesus didn't look glorious on the cross.) "One deserves to be called a [true] theologian," Martin wrote, "who sees God even in suffering." The Bible says that even broken and weak sinners can know God if they trust his word and receive the forgiveness Jesus offers. In fact, Jesus told his disciples that the reason he came to earth was to save sinners (Luke 5:31–32). As Paul wrote, "God chose what is foolish in the world to shame the wise; God chose what is weak in the world to shame the strong; God chose what is low and despised in the world, even things that are not, to bring to nothing things that are" (1 Cor. 1:27–28). This is the message that the theologian of the cross believes. After Heidelberg, the Latin phrase "*Crux sola est nostra theologia*" ("The cross alone is our theology") became a rallying cry for Martin Luther's followers. It still is today.

Martin's students sent his *Heidelberg Disputation* to the printers too. As more of the German people began to read Martin Luther's teaching, they bought fewer indulgences. And when the people stopped spending money on indulgences, Pope Leo began

> ### — Justification by Faith —
>
> Martin Luther taught that Jesus *justifies* all sinners who believe in him. What does this mean? Jesus Christ is the eternal, only begotten Son of God. He was born as a human baby in Bethlehem. Jesus then lived a perfect life and died the painful and shameful death of a cross. Jesus fulfilled all righteousness (Matt. 3:15) and took the punishment due for our sin. God then raised Jesus from the dead, and now declares that in his sight, Jesus's righteous life and sacrificial death count for all who trust in him (Rom. 4:22–25). "Justify" means that God saves and declares believers to be righteous even though we are still sinners (Rom. 5:8). This was Martin Luther's most important teaching. Helping the church remember this truth changed the world.

to take Martin more seriously. Something had to be done about this rebellious German monk.

In October 1518, Martin was summoned to Augsburg, Germany, to meet with a high-ranking church official, Cardinal Thomas Cajetan. *Cardinal* is the title used for church officials who rank just below the pope. The cardinal was a picture of glorious wealth, power, and human learning. The cardinals wear rich, red robes (the bright red birds we call

cardinals are named after these officials), and they have many responsibilities, including choosing a new pope when one dies or retires.

If Martin was afraid when he traveled to Heidelberg, he and his friends were even more afraid when he traveled to Augsburg. The situation was desperate. One hundred years before, a priest named Jan Hus from the nearby region of Bohemia (modern day Czech Republic) had traveled to meet with Catholic leaders like Cardinal Cajetan. Hus had been burned at the stake for teaching doctrines similar to what Martin now taught. Martin was understandably worried. He became so sick to his stomach he was unable to walk.

After some days of rest, Martin recovered enough to meet with the cardinal. Martin's old friend and advisor, Dr. Staupitz, who had traveled with him, encouraged Martin to be respectful. When Martin was brought before Cajetan, he immediately bowed down in front of the fancy chair where the cardinal sat. When Cajetan spoke to Martin, Martin rose to his knees. He only stood when Cajetan asked him to.

The cardinal made his expectations clear. He asked Martin to respond with one simple Latin word, *revoco*, which means "I recant." (To recant means to officially change your mind and reject your earlier ideas.) Instead, Martin politely asked Cajetan to list the errors in his teaching. He wanted to know what he was being asked to reject.

When Cajetan mentioned Martin's teaching about how Jesus justifies sinners, Martin said he couldn't change his mind on that point. To do so would be to reject Christ's cross. Cajetan threatened the priest, "You must recant today, no matter what you wish." He laughed at Martin and asked why he would choose to stand alone against the Catholic Church in all her power and majesty. Cajetan then ended the meeting, "Do not appear before me again until you are ready to recant."

6

I Cannot Recant

1520–1521

JOHANN VON STAUPITZ could see that Martin wasn't getting anywhere by talking to Cajetan. So he encouraged the monk to write out his beliefs and send and appeal directly to Rome. He thought the pope was perhaps misinformed about Martin's actual beliefs. But in January 1520, Pope Leo made it clear that wasn't the case. He issued an official document called a *papal bull*:

> Arise, O Lord, and judge your cause. . . . You have committed the care and rule of your triumphant church to Peter, and the popes as his successors. But now, a wild boar from the forest seeks to destroy it.

The pope who loved to hunt was calling Martin Luther a "wild boar from the forest." Leo was asking God to hunt Martin down. It had only been three years since Martin posted the *Ninety-Five Theses* on Wittenberg's Castle Church door. But in that time, the conflict between Martin, his followers, and the Catholic Church had grown out of control.

Martin had no other options. In that time, the pope had lots of influence over governments across Europe. So when Pope Leo rejected Martin's teaching, he also made the monk an outlaw. The papal bull said Martin must reject his beliefs or else be removed from the church and condemned to death.

I CANNOT RECANT

How did Martin Luther respond? By writing more books! In the fall of 1520, he published three books that became some of his most famous. He wrote to the princes, to the people, and to the pope. As he wrote, his popularity with the German people grew, and so did his troubles.

Within one year, Martin's situation would go from difficult to deadly. In 1521, he would stand trial again. This time, Martin and his friends traveled for two weeks to the city of Worms (pronounced VORMS) in western Germany. In Augsburg, Martin had stood trial before Cardinal Cajetan, a high official in the church. In Worms, he would stand and explain his teachings before Emperor Charles V (the Fifth), the most powerful political leader in all Europe. Charles was king of Spain, and he also ruled the Holy Roman Empire, which included territories that stretched across France and Germany and even down to Italy.

Martin was determined to have more courage in this debate than he did before Cajetan. He told his friend George Spalatin, "Before I said the pope is Christ's servant. Now I declare the pope is Christ's enemy and an apostle of the devil." One thing that helped Martin's confidence was the backing he received from the German people. When Martin arrived in Worms

> ### — Luther's 1520 Trilogy —
>
> **Address to the Christian Nobility** (August 1520). Martin had trained to be a lawyer. He knew how to use crisp, logical arguments when writing to government leaders. Martin argued that every Christian is a priest (1 Pet. 2:9) and no one is higher or lower before God. So the pope can't say he's the only person qualified to explain the Bible. Martin wanted to make clear that the pope had no authority over the German people. The **princes** should stand up to Rome.
>
> **The Babylonian Captivity of the Church** (October 1520). Here Martin spoke directly to the German **people** with these shocking words: "The papacy is identical with the kingdom of Babylon and the

on April 16, two thousand people met him at the city gates. More poured into the streets to greet him with cheers. When he arrived in his room, even some of the German princes came to pledge their support.

> Anti-Christ itself." In the Old Testament, the Babylonians captured the Jews and took them from Jerusalem into exile. In the same way, Martin said, the pope had captured the church and taken it away from Scripture.
>
> ***The Freedom of a Christian*** (November 1520). Martin dedicated this pamphlet to the **pope**. In the introduction, he praised Leo's service to the poor and his godly reputation. But Martin also warned that despite Leo's great wealth and power, he was a slave without Christ. Martin wanted the pope (and all his readers) to see that the gospel sets a Christian free *from* earning his salvation through works. It also sets a Christian free *to* love God and neighbor with a pure heart.

On the next day, April 17, Martin was escorted into the main hall for the trial. Martin was awed by what he saw. Emperor Charles sat on his throne with cardinals and other representatives from Rome around him. Spanish troops decked out in fancy uniforms were stationed around the room, and the crowd watching included bishops, princes, and other powerful German leaders. In the center of the great hall was a table. On it sat a high pile of Martin Luther's books.

An examiner began to read the titles aloud, and then he asked Martin, "Did you write these?"

Martin's confidence started to melt away. He spoke so quietly the people in the hall could hardly hear him, "The books are all mine."

"Will you recant what you've written?"

Recant? What about explaining? Shocked that there wouldn't be a debate and terrified that the emperor would sentence him to death, Martin asked for time to consider his answer. He was given one day.

Martin prayed all night. Then, on the next day, he entered the hall again. There the examiner asked the

I CANNOT RECANT

same questions, "Are these books yours? Will you recant?" This time, Martin didn't feel as overwhelmed. He'd prepared his answer.

> Unless I can be instructed and convinced with evidence from the Holy Scriptures or with open, clear reasoning, I cannot. My conscience is held captive to the word of God. I cannot and will not recant.

Martin stood firm, but with the world against him, no one knew how much longer he'd be able to stand.

7

A Bible for the People
1521–1522

PRINCE FREDERICK of Wittenberg did not want his university's best professor to be killed, but he knew there was a real threat. Even before Martin had gone to Worms, Prince Frederick already guessed that he would be condemned by the emperor.

After the trial, Martin was given twenty-one days

to change his mind. If he didn't recant, his books were to be burned, and he was to be turned over to the authorities right away. If Martin was going to survive this verdict, he would need his prince's help. So Frederick made a plan.

A BIBLE FOR THE PEOPLE

Martin and his friends left Worms and traveled east toward home in Wittenberg. When they came near the woods outside the village of Eisenach, they were suddenly surrounded.

A group of men on horseback drew their swords, and one demanded, "Where's Martin Luther?"

Before one of Martin's friends could answer, another horseman grabbed Martin by his cloak and threw him to the ground. The kidnappers put Martin on the back of one of their horses and immediately darted off into the woods.

Most people thought Martin had been killed, but Prince Frederick had arranged the "kidnapping" to keep Martin safe. Martin was held in protective custody at Wartburg Castle (nicknamed "the Wartburg"), a tall, stone castle that looms high above the wooded hills of the Thuringian Forest. Martin hid in the dark, gloomy fortress for almost ten months.

As long as Martin was at the Wartburg, the pope and the emperor's officials couldn't find him. But Martin had other enemies. Ephesians 6:12 says,

"For we do not wrestle against flesh and blood, but against . . . the spiritual forces of evil." Alone in the castle tower, the devil's accusations filled Martin's mind: *Are you the only wise person? Has the church in so many centuries gone wrong? What if you are wrong about justification? What if you are taking many people with you to hell?*

The old storm in Martin's heart returned. He was depressed and couldn't sleep. Then he remembered Dr. Staupitz's advice to hold on to Christ, to stop thinking about himself, and to serve God's people. He remembered his mentor's words, "You will be a teacher of the Bible."

What better way to teach God's word than to give the German people a Bible that they could read in their own language? There had been German Bible translations before Martin, but these older versions were difficult for regular people to read. What was the point in using fancy and complicated words that couldn't be understood? Martin told his friend George Spalatin, "Give us simple words and not

— How Martin Luther Studied the Bible —

Martin didn't only want people to read the Bible. He wanted them to study it too. "God himself lives in the Bible," Martin wrote. "Therefore, worthy Christian: get in, get in!" Martin had three rules for digging into God's word (each named with a Latin term):

Prayer (*oratio*)—"Kneel down in your private room and with humility, pray to God to give you his Holy Spirit to enlighten and guide and give you understanding."

Meditation (*meditatio*)—"Read and reread the very words written down in the Bible. Observe and think about what the Holy Spirit means. Like David wrote in Psalm 119, you must speak, think, talk, hear, and repeat God's word day and night."

Suffering (*tentatio*)—"As soon as you begin to know God's word, the devil will afflict you and make a real theologian of you. This suffering will teach you how right, true, sweet, lovely, mighty, and comforting God's word is. It is wisdom supreme."

those of the court or castle, for this book should be famous for its simplicity."

To make his translation, Martin studied hard to understand a Bible passage's meaning. He also looked at each verse and thought, *How would a German person say something like that?* Martin wrestled, for example, with Luke 1:28, where the angel Gabriel greeted Mary and announced that she was pregnant with baby Jesus. Some Bible versions had translated his words, "Hail Mary, full of grace." Martin thought this was confusing: "A German can talk about a purse full of gold or a barrel full of beer, but how would a German understand a girl 'full of grace'?" Martin thought that translation missed the point. "I'd prefer to say simply, '*Leibe Maria*' ["beloved Mary"]. What word is richer than that word, '*liebe*'?"

The translation work was humbling for Martin. He wrote, "I have undertaken to translate the Bible into German. This was good for me. If I hadn't done it, I might have died thinking I was smart." Though the work was difficult, Martin completed translating the entire New Testament from its original Greek into German in just eleven weeks.

Martin's time in the Wartburg settled the thunder roaring in his soul. It also prepared him for a different storm. Within the year, he'd return to Wittenberg, ready to face the troubles that raged there.

> **— Martin Luther Was Not Afraid of Ghosts —**
>
> Martin Luther liked to tell stories about the ghosts he heard banging around, knocking and tapping, when he was alone hiding at Wartburg Castle. One day, Martin purchased some fresh hazelnuts for a snack. That night, he woke up because something in the dark was throwing the hazelnuts at him. On another night, Martin was kept awake by what sounded like large beer barrels crashing down the tower stairs.
>
> Martin was also fond of Bible passages that mention ghosts. Every year on the Tuesday after Easter, the church read these words: "As they were talking

about these things, Jesus himself stood among them, and said to them, 'Peace to you!' But they were startled and frightened and thought they saw a spirit [or ghost]" (Luke 24:36–37). Then Martin stood to preach saying, "For the sake of the children, we must say a little something about spirits, because the Gospel reading mentions them."

Martin didn't believe ghosts were wandering human souls like some people do. Instead, he said, "They're either evil spirits who terrify, or angels who bring good news. You shouldn't think that the souls of your loved ones wander the earth." It's good to know this, lest we think evil spirits are hundreds of miles away from us. "Wherever we go, wherever we stand," said Martin, "we are between angels and demons."

Does it feel scary to think that we're always standing among spiritual beings? Martin Luther wasn't scared. He taught Christians how to handle ghosts. Step 1: Pray to Jesus, entrusting yourself to his care. Step 2: Shout about your salvation, or shout a Bible verse with confidence. Step 3: Believe that what God says in his word is true.

When noisy evil spirits pestered Martin with hazelnuts and crashing beer barrels, he commended himself to Jesus's care, shouted "You [God] have put all things under his [Jesus's] feet" (Ps. 8:6), and then went back to bed.

* Adapted with permission from Todd R. Hains, "Martin Luther Is Not Afraid of Ghosts," *Bible Study Magazine* 11, no. 6 (Sept.–Oct. 2019): 8–11.

8

Years of Trouble

1522–1524

MARTIN LUTHER LOOKED UP from the letter he'd received. The Wartburg was still and quiet, but the letter told him things were different back home.

I must see what's happening in Wittenberg with my own eyes, he thought.

That night, Martin crept quietly down the tower

stairs to the stables below. In a wink, he was on a horse and riding out into the cold December night. Martin now had a full head of hair and a beard. If you'd seen him wearing his dark cloak with a sword at his side, you would have thought he was a knight, not a monk.

The day before he arrived in Wittenberg, there had been a riot in the town. Students and townsfolk carrying knives burst into City Church, snatched the service books from the altar, and drove out the priests. They threw stones at any Catholic church members saying prayers to Mary.

The violence troubled Martin. He had used bold language in his books. He'd mocked and insulted Pope Leo, Prince Albert, Johann Tetzel, and others. But his actions had always been gentler than his words. Now he worried that the people were taking his words too far. After visiting Wittenberg secretly, Martin returned to Wartburg Castle. There he wrote a letter to the Christians back in Wittenberg: "There is no reason for riots and rebellion. They almost always harm the innocent more than the guilty. . . . Preach, pray, but do not fight!"

Martin was concerned about rioting mobs, but he was more concerned about the church leaders who stirred them up. While Martin had been away, theology professor Andreas Karlstadt led the reformation efforts in Wittenberg. Sadly, his actions were as brash as Martin's mouth.

Karlstadt didn't guide people to the truth. He pushed them. For example, Karlstadt hated how the Catholic Church practiced the Lord's Supper. The Catholic Church teaches that the bread and wine of the Lord's Supper transform into Jesus's body and blood. To keep from accidentally spilling Jesus's blood, Catholic priests would give only the bread to church members. Karlstadt knew that isn't what the Bible teaches. So, on Christmas Day 1521, he changed everything about the Lord's Supper service. Instead of wearing traditional robes, Karlstadt dressed like a peasant. He didn't say the prayers in the usual Latin; he spoke in German.

And though many church members were afraid, he forced the people to take both the bread and the wine at Communion.

> ## — Luther's Insults —
>
> Martin is famous for his harsh and vivid language. Here are some examples of his sharp pen.
>
> - **To Jerome Emser, a supporter of the pope:** "I should call a barrel-maker and have him put hoops around your head, so it doesn't burst from too much nonsense!"
> - When a prince named **Duke Henry** claimed that Martin made up new doctrines, Martin called him "*Hans Wurst*" or "Johnny Sausage," the German name for a carnival clown who wore a fat sausage through his belt.
> - **To the scholar Erasmus:** "Are you ignorant of what it means to be ignorant?"
> - **To the pope:** "I can with good conscience call you a farting donkey and an enemy of God."

Professor Karlstadt was glad to defy the Catholic Church. A few weeks later, he announced he was leaving the monastery and getting married. Martin supported him. In fact, Martin supported many of the changes Karlstadt made. They were exactly what he'd already written in his books. It wasn't Karlstadt and his followers' views but their rebellious attitude that made Martin worry. Mobs continued to disturb traditional Catholic services. In one riot, they dismantled an altar and burned the church's artwork.

Then more fuel was thrown on the fire. Two days after Christmas, three men arrived in Wittenberg from the southern German town of Zwickau. They claimed to be prophets and said they didn't need the Bible because they had the Holy Spirit. These wild men taught that God would set up his kingdom in Germany if the people would only take up their swords and fight against their Catholic enemies. By mid-February, with the threat of violence increasing, city officials sent a letter to Martin. He was a wanted man, but things in Wittenberg were getting out of hand. It was time for Martin to come home.

On March 9, the people crowded into Castle Church in Wittenberg. Martin Luther was back. The people were eager to hear him preach, but when he taught, they were shocked at what he said: "Of all the enemies who opposed me, I've never felt as much heartache as with you, my friends." Rome had forced Christians to fast, to confess their sins to a priest, and to eat only the bread during Communion. Now the Wittenbergers were doing the same thing. They'd rejected the old law and set up a new one. The only difference was that they were forcing the people to do the opposite of what Rome demanded. Martin rebuked them, "Faith without love is not enough. Indeed, it's no faith at all. . . . Love does not coerce others. Love serves them."

Martin hadn't forced anyone to believe the gospel. The Wittenberg mobs shouldn't either. Martin told the people, "I simply taught, preached, and wrote God's word. . . . I did nothing. The word did

YEARS OF TROUBLE

everything." With Martin back home, Wittenberg calmed down. God's word restored order there, but not everywhere.

Andreas Karlstadt left Martin and became a preacher in Orlamünde, Germany. There he introduced the same changes that caused the uproar in Wittenberg. Karlstadt never approved of violence, but he wrote books criticizing traditional worship, church art, and Martin Luther's views on baptism and the Lord's Supper.

In Bohemia, a fiery preacher named Thomas Müntzer gathered a large following of anti-Catholic reformers who threatened more and more violence. Martin called radicals like Karlstadt and Müntzer "*Schwärmgeister*" (SHVERM-guy-stur is German for swarming spirits). These extremists were like a beehive gone mad! How could they be stopped?

Two years later, in 1524, disease and hunger began to spread across the German countryside. In their suffering, the German peasants (that is the lower-class farmers, shopkeepers, and miners) became fed up with the nobles' greed. When a noblewoman in southern Germany demanded that the peasants in her territory pick strawberries for a great banquet, they rebelled. Soon others in nearby villages followed their example. At first, Martin supported the peasants. They had asked the nobles for the freedom to elect their own pastors. They wanted to fish and hunt in public lakes and forests without charge, and they demanded that the nobles no longer compel them to work for free. Martin could see that these demands were just.

Then, once more, leaders like Thomas Müntzer and a pastor from Switzerland named Ulrich Zwingli began to encourage the peasants to be violent in what became known as the Peasants' War. Müntzer told his followers that God's Spirit had assured him they'd be victorious. Martin couldn't stand to see God's word used to promote rebellion against the government authorities, so he responded with angry words: "The peasants must be sliced, strangled, stabbed, and killed like rabid dogs." Soon after, the

German nobles sent an army to slaughter Müntzer's eight thousand. Müntzer himself was killed in his bed. Across Europe, more than one hundred thousand peasants—men, women, and children—died. After the war, when he saw all the violence and death, Martin called the nobles "senseless tyrants, bound for hellfire." But sadly, they had done exactly what Martin had written.

— People in Luther's Life —

Nicolaus von Amsdorf (nee-KOH-laus fon AHMS-dorf), 1483–1565—Martin's friend who taught theology in Wittenberg. He could have married Katharina von Bora (see chapter 9).

Prince Albert of Brandenburg, archbishop of Mainz (MYNZ), 1490–1545—power-loving ally of the pope who allowed indulgence sales in Germany (see chapters 4, 5, and 9).

Katharina von Bora (kah-tah-REE-nah fon BOH-rah), 1499–1552—runaway nun who married Martin Luther (see chapter 9).

Cardinal Thomas Cajetan (kah-YEH-than), 1469–1534—high-ranking Catholic official who interviewed Martin in Augsburg (see chapters 5 and 6).

Andreas Karlstadt (an-DRAY-us KARL-shtat), 1486–1541—theology professor who oversaw the brash changes in Wittenberg while Martin was at the Wartburg. He took shelter in Martin's home during the Peasants' War (see chapter 8).

Frederick the Wise, 1463–1525—prince of Wittenberg who hid Martin Luther at the Wartburg (see chapter 7).

Pope Leo X (the Tenth), 1475–1521—originally named Giovanni di Lorenzo de' Medici (Gee-oh-VAH-nee dee loh-REHN-zoh deh MEE-dee-chee), this pope wasted the church's money on gambling and hunting parties. He loved to hunt both wild boar and Martin Luther (see chapters 4, 5, and 6).

Philip Melanchthon (mel-AHNK-tohn), 1497–1560—Wittenberg's first professor of Greek. In 1521, he wrote the *Loci Communes*, a systematic summary of Lutheran theology. In 1530, he wrote the Augsburg Confession, the official doctrinal statement of the Lutheran Church. Melanchthon was Martin's most trusted theological advisor, and he remained by Martin's side until Martin's death (see chapters 10, 11, and 12).

Thomas Müntzer (MYOON-tser), 1489–1525—fiery preacher who stirred up violence during the German Peasants' War (see chapter 8).

George Spalatin (spah-LAH-teen), 1484–1545—secretary to Prince Frederick the Wise who carried letters back and forth to Martin Luther while he was "imprisoned" in the Wartburg (see chapters 6 and 7).

Johann von Staupitz (yo-HAHN fon SHTOW-pits), 1460–1524—leader of the Augustinian order who told Martin he would teach the Bible (see chapters 3, 5, and 6).

Johann Tetzel (TET-sel), 1465–1519—wild indulgence preacher who said, "When a coin in the coffer rings, a soul from purgatory springs" (see chapter 4).

Ulrich Zwingli (OOL-reek TSVING-lee), 1484–1531—Swiss pastor who debated with Martin about the Lord's Supper (see chapters 8 and 11).

9

The Estate of Marriage

1523–1534

ONE BRIGHT SPRING MORNING, a fish merchant's wagon rolled down the dirty streets of Wittenberg. The cart was piled high with supplies for the Easter feast. No one was surprised to see the merchant make his normal stop in front of the Black Cloister monastery, where Martin still lived. But they were shocked by what they found hiding in the cargo: twelve runaway nuns!

The nuns were running to freedom. The Catholic Church told people they could earn God's approval if they chose a life without marriage. That's one reason so many young boys and girls during Martin's time became monks and nuns.

THE ESTATE OF MARRIAGE

It can be good to serve God without the distraction of having a spouse or family, but this choice does not earn God's grace. No, Martin Luther taught that God saves people by faith alone. As Martin's teaching spread, thousands of monks and nuns left to serve God outside the monasteries. Many of these men and women came to Wittenberg.

What would Martin do with the twelve young women who had arrived in the wagon?

"I will first inform their families and ask if they will take them in," he said. "If they refuse, I will try my best to find homes where they can live. Several people have already offered. If possible, I would also like to marry a few off."

Martin's plan mostly worked. Yet there was one young woman he couldn't seem to get rid of. Her name was Katharina von Bora, or Katie for short. While Katie waited for suitors to propose marriage, she lived with a local judge's family and worked as a housemaid for Wittenberg's woodcut artist Lucas Cranach. Cranach ran a print shop and a pharmacy, and he always had traveling painters staying at his house. Katie had already studied nursing while she was a nun, but at the Cranach's shop she also learned what it takes to run a small business. Katie had a brilliant mind, and she developed a reputation for speaking her mind.

"She's a lively lady," Martin told a friend. "She's also proud and snooty. I don't know what devil would want to put up with her." It turns out that devil would be Martin himself.

After almost a year and two potential suitors who didn't work out, Katie told Martin's friend Nicolaus von Amsdorf that she would only marry one of two people—Amsdorf himself or Martin Luther. Katie may have meant that as a joke, but Martin took her seriously. On June 13, 1525, they were married, and then two weeks later they celebrated the marriage publicly at the City Church.

At first, Martin thought Katie was arrogant, but soon he grew to love her affectionately. When he would wake up in the morning and see her, he'd say, "Look at this person, the most beautiful creature from God that Christ has given me. To him be all praise and honor. . . . I would not exchange Katie for France or for Venice."

Martin would call Katharina "my Katie," "my boss," and "my Eve." When he was joking with her, he'd even make a pun with her name and call her "my *Kette*," which in German means "my chain." Later in life, when he told his students how much he loved the apostle Paul's letter to the Galatians, he affectionately said, "I love it like my Katharina von Bora."

Martin's love grew, but married life did require some changes. "Before I was married, I did not make my bed for more than a year," he confessed. Katie made him clean house, and she also helped him balance the family budget.

If it had all been up to him, Martin would have given all his money away. Luke 6:38 says, "Give, and it will be given to you." Martin Luther believed that verse. He even gave away money he needed to pay his bills. But that didn't bother him because he hated keeping track of bills. He let Katie deal with the misery of money: "I do not worry about debts because as soon as Katie pays one bill, another comes." Once he declared, "I am never working with money again. I only end up being sad."

Katie, on the other hand, was a wise saver. When the two were married, the pope's old ally, Prince Albert, amazingly sent the couple a wedding gift of

THE ESTATE OF MARRIAGE

twenty guilders—an amount equal to two and half years' salary. Martin didn't want to take money from his sworn enemy. So he told Katie to send it back. Instead, she hid the money in the kitchen pantry and used it to pay their bills.

After their wedding, Katie moved into the Black Cloister, and she worked hard to make it a home. The cloister was a long building with lots of narrow rooms meant to be little bedrooms for monks. The city moat was at one end of the house, and a graveyard was at the other. To raise a family in that building, changes would need to be made. Katie put in a room for washing clothes, waterproofed the house on the moat side, purchased equipment for brewing beer, and had stalls built for pigs, cows, goats, peacocks, and chickens. She also planted a garden in the graveyard, where she grew lettuce, cabbages, peas, beans, melons, and cucumbers. New growth among the dead!

When the church and university in Wittenberg gave Martin a raise in his salary, Katie used the money to buy her old childhood home and farm in Zuhlsdorf as well as an orchard outside Wittenberg where she grew apples, grapes, pears, nuts, and peaches. Martin was very proud of Katie and all the amazing things she did. When he traveled to preach, he would write home to "Her majesty, Lady Katharina von Bora and Zuhlsdorf, my sweetheart," or "Lord brewer, gardener, and whatever else she can do!" Katie's work also included big house projects. It seemed the Luthers' home was always under construction. Over the years of their marriage, Katie added windows, a proper bathroom, and a spring for bringing fresh water to the garden. During one renovation, a wall caved in and nearly crushed Martin!

Did Martin and Katie really need such a large house? Yes! Between children, students, family, and guests, the Luther home was always full. Martin and Katie had six children—Johannes "Hans" (June 7, 1526), Elisabeth (December 10, 1527), Magdalena "Lena" (May 4, 1529), Martin (November 9, 1531), Paul (January 29, 1533), and Margaretha (December 17, 1534). The Luthers also had long-term guests. In those days, it was common for university students to live at their professors' houses when school was in session. (Katie wanted to charge them rent, but Martin often let them stay for free.) After Martin's two sisters died, the Luthers also raised their nephews and nieces. Most days, there were

> ## — Tölpel, Luther's Dog —
>
> Martin Luther had a dog he loved very much. His name, Tölpel (TURL-puhl), means "foolish clown" in German. Martin mentions his dog quite a lot in *Table Talk*, a book of his dinner-table conversations that were written down by the students who lodged in his home. Martin didn't believe that animals have eternal souls, but he did say there will be dogs in heaven: "[God] will create a new heaven and a new earth. He'll also create new [Tölpels], with skin of gold and hair with pearly curls." Martin also saw Tölpel as an example for prayer. "Oh, if I could only pray the way this dog watches the meat! All his thoughts are concentrated. . . . Otherwise, he has no thought, wish, or hope."

seventeen children in the Luther home. Katie, Martin's "morning star of Wittenberg," would get up and start her chores each day at four o'clock in the morning. If she'd begun preparations any later, she wouldn't have been able to feed everyone at the dinner table.

Martin enjoyed his guests, but he loved being a father. He often bragged about his children in his letters: "Hans is teething and beginning to make a joyous nuisance of himself. These are the joys of marriage of which the pope is not worthy." And when Hans was older, Martin wrote him a sweet letter, encouraging him to be diligent with his studies. In the letter, Martin compared heaven with a playground.

> My dear son, I know a lovely place where children joyfully sing, dance, and play. There are apples, pears, cherries, and plums under the trees. You can go to that playground for free if you pray, study, and trust the Lord.

As Martin and Katie built their home and taught their children, they also prayed that God would build his church throughout Germany and the world. But how, Martin wondered, were the churches faring in the German villages outside Wittenberg?

— The Lutheran Rose —

Use colored pencils to shade in the Lutheran Rose (the Luthers' family crest):

Cross: Black for the sins placed on Jesus

Heart: Red for the life of faith

Rose: White for joy

Background: Blue to show that this joy belongs to our heavenly future

10

Hymns and Catechism

1527–1535

BEFORE THE REFORMATION, a Roman Catholic bishop would visit each church under his care at least once every five years. But now that all the churches in Saxony (the wider area around Wittenberg) were Lutheran, those visits had stopped. There were thirty-eight churches that served the villages and

MARTIN LUTHER

farms in that region. No church leaders had visited them for nearly a decade. How were things going? No one in Wittenberg knew.

So, in 1527, Professor Philip Melanchthon put together a plan to investigate. With approval from the prince of Saxony, Martin and Philip sent teams of pastors and teachers from Wittenberg to visit those churches. The visitors traveled across the countryside, attended church services, and asked each pastor about his church's teaching, its style of worship, its finances, and the people's behavior. Martin Luther served on one of the visiting teams. What he saw in the country churches shocked him.

"Dear God, what misery I beheld," Martin wrote. It seemed like everywhere he looked, the churches were in terrible condition. One church building had a leaky roof. Water had dripped in and ruined all the books in the church library. So Martin told the people in the village to take up a collection and make repairs right away. In another town, the visitors found a man who was pastoring two churches—one Lutheran church in Saxony and one Catholic church across the border in a region that was still influenced by the pope. *This is completely unacceptable*, Martin thought, and he told the man he couldn't preach at the Lutheran church any longer.

In the Saxon countryside, Martin also found do-nothings, drunkards, wife-beaters, and scoundrels. When he returned home, Martin wrote down his dismay over what he saw:

> These common people have no knowledge whatever of Christian teaching, and unfortunately many pastors are quite unfit. Although the people are supposed to be Christian, are baptized, and receive the Holy Sacrament, they do not know the Lord's Prayer, the Creed, or the Ten Commandments. They live as if they were pigs and irrational beasts.

What could be done to help the ordinary Saxon people learn to follow Jesus? They had read Martin

Luther's books. Now, they needed to experience a *reformation*.

First, Martin encouraged the people with music. In 1523, he had published a small booklet on how to lead a worship service. The next year, he sent the printer a songbook with twenty-three new hymns he'd composed. When the prince of Wittenberg couldn't afford to pay the church's professional musicians, Martin organized voluntary choirs for adults and children. He also composed music for them. During his lifetime, Martin wrote more than thirty-five songs and hymns. Often the lyrics of his

— **The Reformation** —

The Reformation was the Christian movement that began with Martin Luther and swept across Europe during the 1500s. This movement sought to change (or "reform") the Catholic Church's teaching about salvation and its worship practices.

hymns grew out of the Psalms. Psalm 46:1 says, "God is our refuge and strength, a very present help in trouble." That psalm inspired the 1527 hymn, "A Mighty Fortress Is Our God." It may be Martin's most famous. Around the world, Christians still sing about Christ's victory with these words:

> And though this world with devils filled
> Should threaten to undo us,
> We will not fear, for God hath willed
> His truth to triumph through us.

With his works on worship and music, Martin didn't just teach the people why they should avoid certain Catholic practices, he also showed them how to focus the church's worship on Jesus. Karlstadt's followers had been negative. They had burned church artwork and altars, punishing anyone who wasn't faithful to the Bible. Martin, by contrast, was positive. He used a carrot instead of a stick. He didn't want to lecture the people into obeying God. He wanted to inspire them to obey. Martin played the lute (an instrument like a guitar), and he loved to sing. "Music is a fair and lovely gift of God, which has often moved me to joy," he wrote. "Next after theology, I give to music the highest place and deepest honor."

When Martin returned to Wittenberg after touring Saxony, he also found a second way to make God's truth easy to remember. In addition to songs, he also wrote his *Small Catechism*. (A catechism is a set of simple questions and answers to teach common people and children the basics of Christian faith.) In addition to family prayers and household responsibilities, Martin Luther's catechism had four main sections: the Ten Commandments, the Apostles' Creed, the Lord's Prayer, and the Sacraments (baptism and the Lord's Supper). Here's the question and answer for the first commandment:

You shall have no other gods before me. (Ex.20:3)

Question: What does this mean?
Answer: We are to fear, love, and trust God above all things.

Martin wanted basic truths like this to be on the heart of every Christian in Germany. That included his own heart. "I am still like a child who is being taught the catechism," he wrote. "Every morning I read a section aloud word for word. . . . I still need to study these truths every day."

— Prayer and a Haircut —

One day, Martin Luther went to get his hair cut, and his barber, Peter Beskendorf, asked him a sincere question, "How do you pray?" When Martin got home, he wrote his barber a letter to answer the question more fully. "Dear Master Peter, I will tell you as best I can what I do when I pray. May our dear Lord grant to you and to everybody to do it better than I!" Here is what Martin wrote:

> I make prayer the first business of the morning and the last at night. I say the Ten Commandments, the Creed, and the Lord's Prayer

Martin prepared a version of his catechism in German for families to use at home and another in Latin for schoolteachers because that was the language children learned in school. He reminded parents, and especially fathers, to be faithful in teaching God's word to their children. For Martin, family

> quietly to myself as any child might do. Then, when my heart has been warmed by these truths, I give God thanks for his mercy and begin to pray the Lord's Prayer again slowly, thinking deeply about the meaning of each line. I let my heart be stirred and my requests guided by the words of the Prayer. Know you are not praying alone. All faithful Christians throughout the world also pray the Lord's Prayer with you. Finally, you must always say the amen firmly. Say, "Very well, God has heard my prayer; this I know as a certainty and a truth." That is what "amen" means.

was important. When giving his lectures on Genesis, Martin famously compared the Christian home to a school and a church. He said that a father "is a bishop and priest in his house." Martin wanted mothers and fathers to know that everything they did to care for their children mattered—even changing a baby's diapers.

Martin taught and sang with his own children too. By 1535, Martin's oldest, Hans, was nine, and his youngest, Margaretha, was one. That year, their dear father wrote a song for them. He put the words of the Christmas angels into these easy-to-sing words:

> From heaven on high I come to you,
> And I am bringing you good news.
> So very much good news I bring,
> It makes me want to shout and sing.

The song demonstrates a truth that Martin Luther—in both his hymns and his catechism—deeply believed: The highest theology is the simplest. We must become like children to grasp it.

— Merry Christmas *for You* —

Martin Luther loved Christmas. He preached about it, wrote a Christmas pageant, and composed two Christmas hymns. He's even credited with inventing the Christmas tree. As the legend goes, Martin was walking home one winter evening. He was captivated by the bright stars beautifully shining through the evergreen trees, and he wanted to recreate the scene for his family. So he put up a tree in the main room of his house, gathered the kids around, and tied lighted candles to the branches. We can only imagine what Katie thought about the fire hazard!

Martin rejoiced in Christmas because the holiday beautifully demonstrates God's love and grace. In a sermon Martin preached on Christmas Day, 1530, he said that the big truths we celebrate on Christmas—that the Christ child was born of a virgin to be our Lord and Savior—are not merely facts. They must be received personally. "Even the devil himself can believe the *facts* of Christmas," he said, "but the best news of Christmas is that Jesus not only came in human flesh in Bethlehem. He also came *for you*."

11

Chalk on the Table

1529

IN OCTOBER OF 1529, a group of church leaders met for a colloquy—a great debate—about the Lord's Supper. They gathered at Marburg Castle, which towered high above the winding Lahn River. This time it wasn't the Reformers against Rome. Reformers were fighting among themselves.

Inside the tall, stone castle, a wooden table sat in the center of a great hall. On one side stood the Lutherans: Martin Luther, Philip Melanchthon, and their friends. On the other stood the Reformers from Switzerland and southern Germany: Ulrich Zwingli,

> — **Famous Meetings with Strange Names** —
>
> During his life, Martin Luther debated many people on many topics. Sometimes these debates came to be known by names that sound funny to us today. Here are three of the most famous:
>
> **Diet of Worms** (April 16–18, 1521)—No, they weren't eating earthworms! A "diet" was a meeting where the Holy Roman emperor would meet with his officials. And the German "W" in the name of the city is pronounced like an English "V": *VORMS*. When Martin was brought before the emperor in Worms, he famously said, "I cannot and will not recant" (see chapter 6).

Martin Bucer, and their friends. The prince who called the meeting, his secretary, and several local pastors stood at the room's edges to watch.

They had gathered to debate the meaning of the Lord's Supper. No one in the room wanted to follow

> **Marburg Colloquy** (October 1–4, 1529)—Martin Luther's famous debate with Ulrich Zwingli and Reformed church leaders about the Lord's Supper. "Colloquy" means "a great debate" (see chapter 11).
>
> **Wittenberg Concord** (May 29, 1536)—This "concord" has nothing to do with grapes. (Concord grapes are named after Concord, Massachusetts, the town where they were first grown in 1854.) At the concord in 1536, the Reformed pastor Martin Bucer met with Martin to talk about the Lord's Supper a second time. They reached a concord, an agreement, but when Bucer returned to the Reformed churches, the churches wouldn't accept it.

the pope's views on Communion. The Catholic Church saw the Supper as a sacrifice that would cover the guilt of any righteous people who confessed their sins to a priest. The pope and his followers taught that when a priest blesses the bread and wine, their substance (though not their look and taste) transforms, like magic, into Jesus's body and blood. Then, Jesus's body and blood are re-offered to God as a good work. In this view, what takes away sin isn't what Jesus did on the cross, but the people's work in re-offering the sacrifice. This view is called *transubstantiation*.

Because of this teaching, some people would stand in line to adore the bread and wine before it was served. They thought blessing would come just by looking at it. Others carried pieces of bread to their homes, hoping to plant it in their fields and gardens to receive the blessing of good crops, or to feed it to sick animals to help them get well. To keep from accidentally spilling the enchanted wine, priests gave only the bread to church members, and kept the cup for themselves.

Everyone at Marburg rejected Rome's view of Communion, so they agreed about that much. But what was the right view? They couldn't agree on which teaching about the Supper to adopt in its place. The secretary encouraged the theologians to get along. "The prince's prayer is that all the Reformation churches will stand as one. As you debate, work hard toward brotherly unity. When we finish, we'll sit down at this table and take communion together."

Martin Luther wasn't convinced the debate would end in agreement. Martin had read Zwingli's books. He knew what the Swiss churches taught about the Supper.

Zwingli viewed Communion as little more than a way for believers to obey Jesus. Zwingli emphasized Christ's command to take the Supper "in remembrance of me" (Luke 22:19; 1 Cor. 11:24–25). His teaching is called the *memorial view* of the Supper. Zwingli didn't believe the bread transformed into Jesus's body. That would be impossible. When God the Son came to earth and took on human flesh, he became like humans physically. Zwingli argued that people are limited to *one spot*, so Christ's human body can't be in many locations at the same time when the churches meet to take Communion.

Instead, Zwingli taught that when Jesus said, "This is my body," he thought of the bread and wine as symbols. Jesus meant, "This *represents* my body." When a geography teacher stands in front of a map and says, "This is Switzerland," she knows the image isn't actually the country of Switzerland but only a picture. *It's similar with communion*, thought Zwingli. *Just like the map and the country aren't the same thing, the body of Jesus and the bread can't be the same either*.

Martin despised Zwingli's view. Before the debate, he said, "I would rather drink pure blood with the pope than mere wine with Zwingli." So, as the colloquy began, Martin took a piece of chalk and drew a large circle on the table. Inside the circle, he scribbled Jesus's words from the Gospels in Latin, *Hoc est corpus meum*, "This is my body" (Matt. 26:26). Then, as if these words were the Communion bread itself, Martin dramatically covered them with a linen cloth.

Martin didn't think the bread and wine were magically transformed like the Roman Catholics did. (He hadn't written magic words like *hocus pocus*.) But

Martin did think Jesus meant the words, "This is my body," literally. Martin thought that since Jesus is God, he can be everywhere. So according to Martin's view, it was no problem that at the Lord's Supper, God somehow gave sinners "the true body and blood of our Lord Jesus Christ under the bread and wine." This view is called *sacramental union*.

Martin rejected Zwingli's teaching that Jesus's body could only be in one spot. He accused Zwingli

> ### — Four Views of the Lord's Supper —
>
> Bruce Wayne became Batman after his parents' tragic death. Peter Parker gained his spidey sense from a radioactive spider bite. All superheroes have unique backstories that help us understand them. The same is true with Christian denominations. The backstory told in this chapter helps us understand the major views of the Lord's Supper we find in churches today. Here's a chart to help you keep track of them. Which view didn't come up in this story?

CHALK ON THE TABLE

What is the view? Who followed it?	What is the Supper?	How is Christ present?	Where is this view taught today?
Transubstantiation Thomas Aquinas	A sacrifice for the righteous	The substance of the bread and wine are transformed into Christ's body and blood.	Roman Catholic and Anglo-Catholic churches
Sacramental Union Martin Luther	A promise of forgiveness for sinners	Christ gives us his true body and blood under the bread and wine.	Lutheran and many Evangelical Anglican churches
Memorial View Ulrich Zwingli*	A sign and symbol for believers	The bread and wine are signs that represent Christ's body and blood.	Many Baptist and Non-denominational churches
Spiritual Presence View John Calvin	A means of grace for the church	Christ is spiritually present in the Supper, not merely as a sign but to accomplish what he promises.	Reformed churches in the Anglican, Congregational, Baptist, and Presbyterian traditions

* After his debates with Luther, Zwingli's view came to be more like Calvin's.

of ignoring biblical texts that describe Jesus's resurrected body as moving through walls and doors. Martin said, "You seek to prove that a body cannot be in two places at the same time. I will not listen to proofs . . . based on arguments derived from geometry." Martin was convinced that Christ gives us his very presence, even if it's extra-dimensional.

Like a game of Ping-Pong, the two theologians argued back and forth for days. Finally, Zwingli cried out, "Show me a Bible text that proves your view." Lifting the linen cloth, Martin pointed to the words he had written when the discussion began: *This is my body*. The words were like a line in the sand. "Here's my text," Martin declared. "It's the only one I need."

At the end of the debate, Martin Luther and Ulrich Zwingli finally wept together and asked forgiveness for the harsh words they'd spoken. They even sat down for a meal at the prince's table. Yet they didn't take Communion together. In their views of the Supper, both Luther and Zwingli remained unchanged.

12

Final Words

1530–1546

MARTIN LUTHER was forty-six years old when Philip Melanchthon and the other Lutheran theologians traveled almost 300 miles from the tiny town of Wittenberg to Augsburg, one of the largest cities in all Germany. When they arrived, the Lutherans presented a written statement of their beliefs to

Emperor Charles V and all the princes who helped him govern his many lands. The new confession of faith was called the Augsburg Confession. Charles V and his Catholic advisors rejected it right away. Yet in an incredible act of defiance, most of the German princes who served under Charles chose to disobey him. They stood with the Lutherans and protested the pope.

Because he was still an outlaw, Martin Luther didn't attend that meeting. Yet he did travel with his friends most of the way, and he stayed close by in Coburg Castle. When he heard the news about what happened in Augsburg, Martin said, "I am tremendously pleased to have lived to this moment when Christ has been publicly proclaimed by his confessors." Martin was tremendously pleased, but he was also filled with grief. Why? On that same day, June 25, 1530, Martin received word that his father had died. When the message came, Martin took a copy of the book of Psalms, went to the castle cellar, and wept. Joy and grief had come together, and Martin sobbed so much he had a headache the next day.

After Augsburg, Charles V was furious with the princes who had rebelled against him. The emperor was already fighting a war with the Ottoman Empire, and the Lutheran princes feared that Charles might send his army to attack them too. These princes prayed for peace, but they also planned for the worst. In February 1537, the princes gathered to make plans in the city of Smalcald. They asked Martin to meet with them and preach to them.

On the way to that meeting, Martin began to feel weak. He preached on the Sunday after he arrived, but he was forced to end his sermon early because he was in pain. For years Martin had been a sick man. He battled headaches, high blood pressure, a weak heart, depression, skin sores, and ringing ears. On this trip, the trouble was a terrible case of kidney stones that kept Martin from urinating. When Philip Melanchthon arrived for the meeting a week later and saw his friend looking green and swollen, he immediately broke down and cried. He thought Martin was going to die.

Everyone prepared for Martin's death. Friends gathered, and the prince of Wittenberg sent his carriage to carry Martin home to Katie. (He thought it would be carrying Martin's dead body.) But after

the carriage traveled ten miles, it stopped at an inn. For the first time in over a week, Martin thought he might be able to relieve himself. Shortly after midnight, he wrote a letter back to Philip in Smalcald. Their prayers had been answered. The kidney stones were gone, so Martin thanked God for his healing:

> Praise be to God the Father of our Lord Jesus Christ, Father of mercy and God of all comfort, who in this late hour of the night has opened my bladder quite unexpectedly.

When the letter arrived in Smalcald, messengers ran through the streets: "Luther lives! Luther lives!" In Augsburg, Martin's joy had been mixed with grief. Now in Smalcald, his sickness and his friends' grief had ended in joy.

Jesus said, "In the world you will have tribulation. But take heart; I have overcome the world" (John 16:33). Martin Luther understood this verse. He had many troubles—Prince Albert, the pope, and even kidney stones. Though each trial tested his faith,

Martin continued to trust in Christ's victory. Yet the most severe trial came five years after Smalcald.

In 1542, Martin's daughter Magdalena fell deathly ill. As her condition worsened, Martin prayed for his Lena: "I love her very much, but if it is your will to take her, dear God, I shall be glad to know she is with you." Though Martin put on a brave face, he was overcome with grief. After kneeling by Lena's bed to comfort her, Martin turned away and quoted Matthew 26:41: My "spirit indeed is willing, but [my] flesh is weak." Lena soon died, and as Martin wept over her body, he expressed his faith that she'd be with Jesus in the resurrection. "Ah, dear child," he said. "You must be raised up and will shine like the stars, yes, like the sun." Though Martin knew this good news was true, he still felt stinging sadness over his daughter's death. He told his students, "It is strange to know that she is surely at peace and that she is well off there, very well off, and yet to grieve so much!"

In February of 1546, Martin Luther heard that some members of his extended family in Mansfeld

— Angry Words —

Martin was zealous and driven. He once said, "When I want to compose, write, pray, and preach well, I must be angry." But while the anger may have given him energy for work, it too often burned out of control.

In 1543, Martin used some of his harshest words to write a document titled *On the Jews and Their Lies*. He had heard that some Jewish rabbis were attempting to convert Lutheran Christians to Judaism. In response, Martin lashed out, "My advice is that their synagogues be burned down . . . that all their books might be taken from them . . . and that they might be forbidden on pain of death to pray publicly in our country." Sadly, Martin's words hurt Jewish people during his lifetime, and his words have also been used to encourage hatred of the Jewish people since that time. Thankfully, the ideas Martin Luther expressed about the Jewish people have been rejected by Lutherans and other Christians worldwide.

were fighting over the family inheritance. Martin was sixty-two years old and by now very sickly. He was a famous author and an important figure in the church. There were lots of reasons for him not to get involved in a family squabble, but still he went. And just like when he traveled to Smalcald, Martin again began to feel weak on the way to Mansfeld. After he arrived in Mansfeld and began to help his family talk through their argument, Martin continued to feel worse and worse.

Finally, the dispute was settled, and Martin collapsed into bed, weary and in pain. In the middle of the night, he woke up and shouted, "Oh, dear Lord! My pain is so great!" Martin knew he was dying. He was probably having a stroke. For two hours, Martin repeated John 3:16: "For God so loved the world, that he gave his only Son, that whoever believes in him should not perish but have eternal life." Then, at three o'clock in the morning on February 18, 1546, Martin Luther died.

Martin had often taught that believers are *simul iustus et peccator*. That is Latin for "declared righteous and sinful at the same time." Both are true of every Christian. Both were true of Martin Luther. Martin battled enemies who wanted him dead, endured a sick and failing body, and fought his own sinful anger until his dying day. He was a broken man who desperately needed God's grace, and he knew it. Before he died, Martin had scribbled out his last written words: "We are beggars. This is true."

Martin knew he could never earn God's grace. Salvation is not won through fasting, indulgences, or daily prayers. This is what Martin Luther had discovered from the Bible and taught again to the world. God sent his only Son. Christ has overcome the world. All he asks of us is that we believe.

Conclusion

Lessons from a Life

WHEN MARTIN LUTHER PUBLISHED his *Ninety-Five Theses*, he started one of the most significant Christian movements in world history—the Protestant Reformation. Martin published hundreds of books, sermons, and hymns. He translated the entire Bible into the language of the common people in Germany. His teaching changed the way poor peasants and rich nobles

CONCLUSION

in Germany related to one another, and it was a major turning point for the church in Europe and throughout the world. It changed what people believed, the way they worshiped, and the way they lived. What made the difference? How did an unknown monk become such a world-changing force? The answer is in the words "the righteousness of God."

Romans 1:16–17 says, "For I am not ashamed of the gospel. . . . For in it *the righteousness of God* is revealed from faith for faith." When he was growing up in school and at the monastery, Martin Luther learned to think about "the righteousness [or justice] of God" as God's *active* judgment against sin. He later wrote, "Though I lived as a good monk and no one could criticize my actions, I felt and knew that I was a sinner before God. I had an extremely disturbed conscience. . . . I hated the righteous God who punishes sinners."

But when Martin was made a university professor and began to study the Bible, he began to see "the righteousness of God" in a new light. Martin saw

CONCLUSION

how Jesus Christ took on our humanity, how he lived a perfect life and died the painful and shameful death of the cross to take the punishment due for sin. Martin saw how God raised Jesus from the dead, and how he now justifies Christians by faith. God declares that in his sight, Jesus's righteous life and sacrificial death count for every believer. In this way, the "righteousness of God" isn't merely his justice or judgment. It's also his gift of salvation.

What happened when Martin made this discovery? Here's how he described it: "Then I felt that I was altogether born again and had entered paradise itself through open gates." After that day, Martin began to teach that God gives Christians his *alien* righteousness. When he used the word "alien," Martin didn't mean that this righteousness comes to us from another planet. What he meant was that the righteousness comes *extra nos*. That's Latin for "from outside of us." Our righteousness isn't from us; it doesn't come from what we do. It can't be earned by purchasing an indulgence, saying a prayer, or even by having a good attitude. Our righteousness is ultimately found in and belongs to another, our Savior Jesus Christ.

In his *Lectures on Galatians*, Martin compared faith to the metal clasp of a ring. He said, "Faith takes hold of Christ, holding on to him like a ring holds its gem." It's not the metal band that gives the ring its worth. The value comes from the diamond the ring holds. In the same way, it's not the strength or size of our faith that saves us. It's Christ outside of us who saves. Christ is our righteousness. We must hold on to him.

Study Questions

Chapter 1: Thunder and a Vow

1. Why did Martin Luther decide to become a monk?

2. Imagine you were in Martin Luther's shoes during the storm. What would you have done or said?

3. Why did Martin think being a monk could help him feel more peace?

Chapter 2: Trembling before the Father

1. What did Martin promise to do when he became a monk?

2. Martin felt scared and worried he couldn't please God. Can you think of a time when you felt worried about

something you did wrong? Or something right you didn't do? How did you handle that feeling?

Chapter 3: He Went for the Saints

1. Why did Martin Luther and his friend travel to Rome? What did they hope to see and do there?

2. What are indulgences, and why did people buy them?

3. How did Martin feel about indulgences before and after his trip to Rome?

4. What assignment did Dr. Johann von Staupitz give to Martin? How did Martin feel about it?

Chapter 4: Coin in the Coffer

1. Why was Pope Leo X's spending a problem for the Catholic Church?

2. How did Prince Albert of Brandenburg help Pope Leo X? What did he want in return?

STUDY QUESTIONS

3. What did Martin begin to learn about forgiveness and salvation? How did his views differ from Pope Leo X and Prince Albert's?

Chapter 5: Theologian of the Cross

1. According to Martin Luther, how is a theologian of the cross different from a theologian of glory? Can you think of an example from everyday life that illustrates these two ways of thinking about God?

2. Why was Martin Luther summoned to meet with Cardinal Thomas Cajetan in Augsburg?

3. What did Dr. Staupitz advise Martin to do during the meeting? What did Cardinal Cajetan want Martin to do? Why did Martin refuse?

Chapter 6: I Cannot Recant

1. How did Pope Leo X describe Martin Luther in his papal bull? Why did Leo write the bull and describe Martin in that way?

STUDY QUESTIONS

2. How did the conflict between Martin Luther, his followers, and the Catholic Church escalate after Martin posted the *Ninety-Five Theses*?

3. Can you list the three books Martin published in 1520? What was each book's message?

4. Why did Martin's situation become more dangerous? Describe how his 1521 trial unfolded.

Chapter 7: A Bible for the People

1. Why did Martin Luther choose to translate the New Testament into German during his time at the Wartburg? How long did it take him to complete this translation?

2. Describe Martin's approach for making a translation understandable for regular people.

3. What were Martin's three rules for studying the Bible?

4. According to Martin Luther, how is suffering connected to understanding God's word?

STUDY QUESTIONS

Chapter 8: Years of Trouble

1. Why did Martin Luther decide to leave Wartburg Castle and return to Wittenberg?

2. Who was Andreas Karlstadt? What changes did he make in Wittenberg while Martin was away?

3. How did Martin react to the rioting mobs and radical leaders who used his teachings to promote violence and rebellion?

4. Why did Martin change his stance on the Peasants' War?

Chapter 9: The Estate of Marriage

1. How did Martin Luther's teachings about marriage differ from the Catholic Church's beliefs during his time? What did Martin believe the Bible teaches about the purpose of marriage?

2. What were some of the qualities that characterized Katharina von Bora? How did Martin Luther initially perceive her?

STUDY QUESTIONS

3. How did marrying Katharina von Bora change Martin Luther? How did Katie change the Black Cloister?

Chapter 10: Hymns and Catechism

1. Why did Professor Philip Melanchthon and Martin Luther send teams of pastors and teachers to visit churches in the Saxon countryside? What did Martin discover during these visits? Why was he shocked?

2. What was Martin Luther's goal with his *Small Catechism*? What were the main sections included in the catechism? Can you find and memorize a question and answer from Martin's *Small Catechism* that was *not* included in this book?

3. Why did Martin Luther find the Christmas holiday so significant and joyous? How did he and his family celebrate Christmas?

Chapter 11: Chalk on the Table

1. What was the purpose of the colloquy held at Marburg Castle in 1529? Who were the main participants on each side of the debate?

STUDY QUESTIONS

2. Describe the Catholic Church's view of the Lord's Supper, including the concept of transubstantiation.

3. What was Martin Luther's perspective on the Lord's Supper, and how did it differ from Ulrich Zwingli's view?

4. What did Martin emphasize about the words, "This is my body" (Matt. 26:26)? Do you agree with him? Which view of the Lord's Supper do you think best fits with what God's word says?

Chapter 12: Final Words

1. What was the Augsburg Confession, and why was it significant?

2. What health challenges did Martin Luther face? How did Martin's health affect his ability to preach and travel?

3. What is the meaning of the Latin phrase *simul iustus et peccator*, and how did Martin Luther apply this concept to himself and other believers?

4. What were Martin Luther's final words? What message about salvation did Martin emphasize with these words?

STUDY QUESTIONS

Conclusion: Lessons from a Life

1. How did Martin Luther initially understand "the righteousness of God" (Rom. 1:17), and how did his view change as he studied the Bible? How did this new understanding affect his relationship with God?

2. Explain the concept of "alien righteousness." Why was it important for Martin Luther?

3. In your own words, describe how faith is like a ring clasp holding a gem.

Timeline

MARTIN LUTHER'S LIFE AND WORLD EVENTS

Year	Events	Age
1397	The Medici Bank established in Florence, Italy.	
around 1440	Goldsmith Johannes Gutenberg invents the moveable-type printing press.	
1483	On November 10, Martin Luther is born to Hans and Margarethe Luther in Eisleben, Germany.	0
1492	King Ferdinand and Queen Isabella expel the Jews from Spain. Christopher Columbus sails west and lands in North America.	9
1504	Michelangelo's *David* installed in a piazza in Florence, Italy.	20
1505	On July 2, caught in a thunderstorm near Stotternheim, Martin Luther vows to become a monk. On July 17, he enters the Augustinian monastery in Erfurt.	21

☐ MARTIN LUTHER'S LIFE ▨ WORLD EVENTS

TIMELINE

Year	Events	Age
1509	Henry VIII becomes king of England.	25
1510	Martin Luther travels to Rome to represent his monastery in a dispute.	26
1511	In the fall, under the pear tree at the Black Cloister in Wittenberg, Johann von Staupitz tells Martin Luther that he will teach the Bible.	28
1512	Michelangelo finishes painting the Sistine Chapel ceiling, commissioned by Pope Julius II in 1508.	29
1513	Giovanni di Lorenzo de' Medici becomes Pope Leo X.	30
1517	On October 31, Martin Luther posts the *Ninety-Five Theses* on the Castle Church door.	33
1518	In the spring, Martin writes the *Heidelberg Disputation* and defends it before leaders of the Augustinian order. In October, he's summoned to Augsburg for interrogation by Cardinal Cajetan.	34
1520	Suleiman the Lawgiver becomes sultan of the Ottoman Empire.	36
1520	In June, a papal bull *Exsurge Domine* ("Arise, O Lord") gives Martin Luther sixty days to recant or be removed from the Catholic Church. In the fall, he writes three major works—*Address to the Christian Nobility* (August), *Babylonian Captivity of the Church* (October), and *The Freedom of a Christian* (November).	36

TIMELINE

Year	Events	Age
1521	Martin Luther refuses to recant before the emperor at the Diet of Worms, and then he goes into protective custody at Wartburg Castle.	37
1522	In March, Martin returns to Wittenberg to calm the turmoil there. In September, he publishes his German translation of the New Testament.	38
1524–1525	The German Peasants' War, the largest uprising of lower-class workers in European history before the French Revolution, is supported by Thomas Müntzer and Ulrich Zwingli.	40–41
1525	In June, Martin Luther marries former nun Katharina von Bora.	41
1528	Martin Luther visits rural Saxony to gather information on the state of religious life there. After the visits, he publishes the *Small Catechism* (May 1529).	44
1530	In June, Philip Melanchthon presents the *Augsburg Confession* at the Diet of Augsburg. The Lutheran princes formally break with the Catholic Church.	46
1536	Anne Boleyn is beheaded in England.	52
1537	In February, Martin Luther attends the conference in Smalcald where he suffers a severe kidney stone attack.	53
1539	Hernando de Soto begins his exploration of North America, looking for the fountain of youth.	55

TIMELINE

Year	Events	Age
1542	Magdalena, Martin Luther's daughter, dies after a painful illness.	58
1543	Martin Luther writes and publishes his angry treatise, *On the Jews and Their Lies*.	59
1545	First meeting of the Council of Trent, the Roman Catholic Church's response to the Protestant Reformation.	61
1546	Martin Luther dies in Mansfeld and is buried at Castle Church.	62
1555	The Peace of Augsburg allows each German state to follow its own religion, and Charles V relinquishes the title of Holy Roman Emperor.	
1738	John Wesley hears Martin Luther's *Preface to the Epistle to Romans* read publicly and finds his heart "strangely warmed."	
1776	On July 4, the Continental Congress unanimously adopts the Declaration of Independence, announcing the American colonies' separation from Great Britain.	
1789	On July 14, an angry mob protesting the monarchy storms the Bastille prison in Paris, France. This act of defiance becomes one of the defining moments of the French Revolution.	
1934	After visiting eastern Germany, Baptist pastor Michael King changes his name to Martin Luther King Sr. and names his young son Martin Luther King Jr.	

More to Explore

IF YOU'D LIKE TO READ MORE about Martin Luther, there are several books that tell the story of his life. Some of the books in the list below are written for younger readers like you. Some of the adult books in the list are challenging to read but worth the effort.

BOOKS TO TRY NEXT

Luther: A Visual Book by Aaron Armstrong and Stephen McCaskell (Patrol, 2017). A beautifully designed and illustrated overview of Martin's life and influence.

Martin Luther: Reformation Fire by Catherine MacKenzie (CF4Kids, 2016). A chapter book overview of Martin's life similar to this book.

The Barber Who Wanted to Pray by R. C. Sproul (Crossway, 2011). A picture book inspired by the true story of Martin Luther and the simple, powerful question his barber once asked him.

ADULT BOOKS YOU MIGHT ENJOY

Here I Stand: A Life of Martin Luther **by Roland H. Bainton (Abingdon Press, 1950).** A very popular introductory biography of Martin Luther and the Reformation generally.

Luther the Reformer: The Story of the Man and His Career **by James M. Kittelson and Hans H. Wiersma (Fortress Press, 2016).** Long considered the standard Luther biography—fair, insightful, and detailed without being overwhelming.

Martin Luther's Basic Theological Writings. **Edited by Timothy F. Lull and William R. Russell (Fortress Press, 2012).** A collection of Martin Luther's writings which can be challenging for adults to read but worth the effort.

Martin Luther: A Spiritual Biography **by Herman Selderhuis (Crossway, 2017).** An award-winning book by a highly respected Reformation scholar, tracing Martin Luther's spiritual journey from his childhood through the Reformation to his influential later years.

Also Available from the Lives of Faith and Grace Series

Perfect for summer reading—or all year round—the Lives of Faith and Grace series will engage kids ages 8–13 with the real-life stories of Christian men and women from history. These short and lively biographies feature pencil sketch illustrations, maps, timelines, bonus sidebars, study questions, and options for further reading.

For more information, visit **crossway.org**.